Inside
AMERICAN POLI

CW00548970

# Executive Orders

By Charlie Samuels

# LUCENT
P R E S S

Published in 2019 by
**Lucent Press, an Imprint of Greenhaven Publishing, LLC**
353 3rd Avenue
Suite 255
New York, NY 10010

For Brown Bear Books Ltd
Editorial Director: Lindsey Lowe
Managing Editor: Tim Cooke
Designer: Lynne Lennon
Design Manager: Keith Davis
Picture Manager: Sophie Mortimer
Children's Publisher: Anne O'Daly

**Picture Credits**
**Front cover:** Pool/Getty Images News/Getty Images
**Interior: Alamy:** Ian Dagnall, 11; **Getty Images:** Ronan Tivorny/NurPhoto, 29; **iStock:** tonda, 31; **Library of Congress:** 7, 8, 10, 12, 14, 17, 18; **Public Domain:** Creative Commons, 28, 34, Pax Ahimsa Gethen, 27, National Portrait Gallery/Google Art Project, 9, NYPL/Bernice Abbott, 16, Gage Skidmore, 38, U.S. Army, 21, U.S. Department of Defense/Navy Petty Officer Michael Billings, 23, U.S Department of Homeland Security/ICE News Media Gallery, 40, U.S. Federal Government/U.S. Air Force, 22, U.S Government Archives/US-Regierun, 20, White House, 30; **Shutterstock:** Drop of Light, 6, Everett Historical, 15, Andrew Flavin, 26, Gina Jacobs, 25, KMH Photography, 43, Lucky-photographer, 5, Sean Pavone, 13, Christopher Penier, 35, Bill Perry, 42, Rena Schild, 39, Joseph Sohm, 4, 24, 32, 37, 45, Karl Sonnenberg, 33, Sorbis, 41, turtix 44.

Brown Bear Books has made every attempt to contact the copyright holders.
If you have any information please contact licensing@brownbearbooks.co.uk

**Cataloging-in-Publication Data**

Names: Samuels, Charlie.
Title: Executive orders / Charlie Samuels.
Description: New York : Lucent Press, 2019. | Series: Inside American politics | Includes glossary and index.
Identifiers: ISBN 9781534566590 (pbk.) | ISBN 9781534566606 (library bound) |
ISBN 9781534566613 (ebook)
Subjects: LCSH: Executive power–United States–Juvenile literature. |
Executive orders–United States–Juvenile literature. | Presidents–United States–Juvenile literature.
Classification: LCC JK517.S26 2019 | DDC 352.23'50973–dc23

Printed in the United States of America

CPSIA compliance information: Batch #BW19KL: For further information contact Greenhaven Publishing LLC, New York, New York at 1-844-317-7404.

Please visit our website, www.greenhavenpublishing.com. For a free color catalog of all our
high-quality books, call toll free 1-844-317-7404 or fax 1-844-317-7405.

# Contents

# Chapter 1

# A STROKE OF THE PEN, THE LAW OF THE LAND

In his first week as president in January 2017, Donald J. Trump issued 14 executive actions, including six executive orders. That beat the previous record of 13 executive actions, set by Barack Obama in his first week as president in January 2009. In both cases, the new president was eager to start delivering on his campaign promises.

*During his presidential campaign, Donald J. Trump criticized politicians for being too slow to take action.*

## Presidential Power

An executive order allows a president to direct **federal agencies** to follow a particular course of action. Executive orders usually have the force of laws. Unlike most laws, however, they do not have to be passed by Congress. Instead, the president simply signs them. An assistant to President Bill Clinton in the 1990s summed up the process by saying, "A stroke of the pen, the law of the land."

Executive orders are an efficient way for a president to avoid being held up by politicians who might oppose his or her wishes. Debating a law in Congress can take months, and the law might not be passed. An executive order can take effect straight away. However, executive orders can be controversial. Critics say that presidents use them in order to avoid rigorous examination of their policies by other lawmakers. Some people are concerned that presidents have used executive orders to expand the power of the executive branch of the government, which is comprised of the president, the **cabinet**, and their staffs. Critics claim that this expansion has weakened the role of the **legislature**. The legislature is comprised of the House of Representatives and the Senate, which together make up the US Congress.

*The US Congress is home to both a main chamber, the House of Representatives, and an upper chamber called the Senate. The two-chamber system is based on the British parliament.*

# The Power of the People

The US Congress has 535 elected representatives, 100 in the Senate and 435 in the House of Representatives. Their role is to debate and vote on new laws. They have no powers to debate executive orders. That does not stop members of Congress from making their views clear. In January 2017, President Trump used an executive order to introduce a ban on immigration from seven mainly Muslim countries. He said the measure was a necessary protection against terrorism. Many people objected that the ban was racist. Members of Congress joined demonstrations against the ban throughout the country. Even legislators from Trump's own Republican Party spoke out about the ban. Although Congress had no vote, many members made sure their opposition to the ban was clear to the electorate and the president.

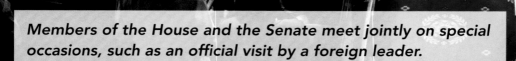

*Members of the House and the Senate meet jointly on special occasions, such as an official visit by a foreign leader.*

All US presidents signed executive orders except William Henry Harrison. The most were signed by Franklin D. Roosevelt, president during the Great Depression of the 1930s and World War II (1939–1945). His 3,721 executive orders included Executive Order 9066 of 1942. It controversially ordered the detention of Japanese Americans in **internment** camps.

The most famous executive action is the Emancipation Proclamation, issued by Abraham Lincoln during the Civil War (1861–1865). The proclamation effectively ended slavery in the United States. It was seen as highly controversial by the Confederates, but it was supported by abolitionists.

*The Emancipation Proclamation was so popular it was illustrated and printed in many versions for collectors to display.*

## WHAT DO YOU THINK?

Executive orders make it possible for the president to make major decisions. Should important questions be decided by one person alone? Does it matter who makes the decision?

# Chapter 2

# WHAT ARE EXECUTIVE ACTIONS?

**P**residents use three types of presidential or executive actions: executive orders, presidential memoranda, and proclamations. These actions have similar effects, with differences of detail.

An executive order is a document that instructs government agencies how to work within overall **policies** set by Congress and the Constitution. The order must explain the Constitutional authority under which it is issued. Executive orders are published in the *Federal Register*, the journal of government proceedings.

A presidential memorandum is like an executive order, but it does not have to spell out the legal authority on which it is based.

*George Washington used the first executive action in 1789. One of his earliest proclamations established the annual Thanksgiving holiday.*

It also does not have to be published. A presidential proclamation is a statement about public policy. It does not have the force of law unless it is authorized by Congress. Most proclamations are symbolic rather than practical. They often establish holidays or recognition of particular causes, such as when President Ronald Reagan proclaimed "Save Your Vision Week" in 1981.

*William Henry Harrison, who was president for just a month in 1841, is the only president not to have issued any executive orders.*

All executive actions are limited in scope. Most importantly, they cannot involve the spending of any money that has not been approved by Congress. Also, they can only direct the actions of federal bodies, not those of private citizens.

## Interpreting the Constitution

The US Constitution does not specifically give the president power to issue executive actions. Instead, the authority is widely accepted as being implied in Article II, which outlines the powers and responsibilities of the president as head of the executive branch of the government and commander in chief of the armed forces. Section 3 of the article includes the phrase, "He shall take Care that the Laws be faithfully executed."

Section 3 is taken as giving the president the authority to instruct federal agencies on the precise manner in which they are to apply laws. However, the clause is only worded loosely. It does not specify what the president may or may not do. This is one of the reasons executive orders are sometimes so controversial.

To some observers, the president's ability to shape government policy contradicts the Constitution. According to the idea of the **separation of powers**, the legislature, or Congress, passes new laws. The role of the executive is to enforce those laws, not to create them. The third branch of government, the **judiciary**, ensures that the laws passed by Congress and the actions of the executive branch are legal.

*Franklin D. Roosevelt signs a bill into law. Roosevelt's frequent use of executive actions delighted his supporters, but greatly upset his political opponents.*

# THE POWER OF THE PEOPLE

Some critics of executive orders argue that the framers of the Constitution did not intend to give any unusual powers to the president. When the Constitution was written in 1787, Americans had recently fought for their freedom from what they saw as the **tyranny** of the British king. The framers therefore avoided giving too much power to any individual. Instead, they gave the power to make laws to elected representatives of the people in the form of Congress. They deliberately tried to ensure that no individual could be powerful enough to begin tyranny like that of Europe's monarchs in the 1700s.

Executive orders can be reviewed by federal courts. If a court rules that an executive order is unconstitutional, it can halt or delay its implementation. Supporters of the use of executive orders say this safeguard prevents a president from acting unlawfully, while enabling him to deliver rapid change. They say this is particularly useful because decision-making in Washington, D.C., is often slowed down by party-political rows and lobbying by special interest groups.

## WHAT DO YOU THINK?

Many people find politics frustrating. Republicans and Democrats often seem to block one another's policies. What ideas do you have that might make political debate more effective?

*In March 1942, Franklin D. Roosevelt issued Executive Order 9096, which reorganized and enlarged the US Navy so that it could fight in the Pacific and Atlantic Oceans at the same time.*

## Commander in Chief

Under the Constitution, the president is also Commander in Chief of the United States. This traditionally gives the president considerable power over military affairs. In the past, this has been of particular importance in wartime, when it might be necessary to make quick decisions. At the start of the Civil War in 1861, for example, Abraham Lincoln used an executive order to bring 75,000 militia members into the Union Army. In World War II, Franklin D. Roosevelt used executive orders to reorganize the US military for the conflict and to call for recruits. He also used executive orders to establish committees to oversee the wartime economy, take over land for military use, and organize the distribution of resources.

## WHAT DO YOU THINK?

Some people believe Franklin D. Roosevelt set out to bring the United States into World War II. According to the Constitution, only Congress can declare war. How might the president's actions be justified?

## Numbering Orders

The earliest executive orders were not numbered. Some were not even recorded after they had been enacted, so there is no way of knowing how many there were or what they concerned. In the early 1900s, however, the State Department began to number all executive orders consecutively. It started retrospectively, giving number 1 to an executive order that had been signed by Abraham Lincoln in 1862. Since the early 1900s, all executive orders have been numbered as they are issued. At the end of 2017, President Donald Trump issued Executive Order 13,819.

*In state governments such as that in Jackson, Mississippi, state governors can issue executive orders that allow measures to be implemented without the approval of the legislature.*

# Chapter 3

# EXECUTIVE ORDERS
# IN HISTORY

Throughout US history, executive actions have been responsible for far-reaching change. One of the most celebrated was Abraham Lincoln's Emancipation Proclamation of 1863.

*Union victory at Antietam encouraged Lincoln to issue the Emancipation Proclamation.*

In July 1862, Lincoln read his cabinet a draft proclamation that would free slaves in Confederate states that did not stop their rebellion by January 1, 1863. That would affect about 3 million African Americans. Before he issued the proclamation, however, Lincoln waited until the North was in a militarily stronger position after the Battle of Antietam in September 1862.

The Emancipation Proclamation outraged people in the South and anti-abolitionists in the North, but it sparked great celebrations among slaves and supporters of **abolition**. Because it was wartime, Lincoln issued the proclamation as Commander in Chief to help impose order on the rebellion.

## The Power of the People

The Emancipation Proclamation went into effect on January 1, 1863. In Confederate states, some plantation owners tried to keep the news from their slaves. When the slaves did hear the news, however, many did not want to wait to be liberated by Union forces. They left their homes and began to make their way toward Union-controlled land. If they arrived there successfully, they were instantly declared free.

*After the Emancipation Proclamation, slave families left plantations carrying all their possessions. They were free, but they were often not welcomed by Union forces.*

*During the Depression of the early 1930s, unemployed Americans lived in cardboard or wooden shantytowns named "Hoovervilles" after the president of the time, Herbert Hoover.*

Partly because of the wartime circumstances, no one challenged Lincoln's power to issue the proclamation. By making the abolition of slavery an official aim of the Union in the war, Lincoln ensured that the Confederacy would not gain recognition from other countries.

## The New Deal

President Franklin D. Roosevelt (FDR) was elected in 1933. After an economic boom in the 1920s, the US economy had crashed in October 1929. Economic crisis spread around the world, causing what became known as the Great Depression. In the United States, workers lost their jobs, people lost their homes, and banks began to fail, destroying people's savings. One reason Roosevelt won the election was his promise of a "new deal" to end economic suffering.

Roosevelt was inaugurated on March 4, 1933. At once he began a program of legislation to try to reassure Americans. On the day of his inauguration he used a presidential proclamation to declare a four-day bank holiday. This gave Congress time to pass an emergency banking act. It also allowed ordinary Americans to settle down and become less panicked.

FDR also signed executive orders to create agencies that would generate work. They included the Civil Works Administration, which created about 4 million government jobs. Another order created an Import/Export bank. In 1934, Roosevelt created the Rural Electrification Administration. Its task was to bring supplies of electricity to rural parts of the country. This move was intended to stimulate the rural economy.

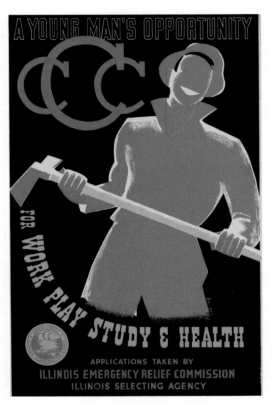

*Agencies such as the Civilian Conservation Corps (CCC) provided work for young people.*

## WHAT DO YOU THINK?

FDR was elected a record four times as president. Some Americans objected that his use of executive power made him a tyrant. Should presidents' terms be limited to restrict their power?

# Japanese Internment

On February 19, 1942, during World War II, FDR signed one of the most controversial of all executive orders. Executive Order 9066 allowed military commanders to designate areas of the country as military areas from which they could exclude "any or all persons." In fact, the military used the order as authority to declare that all Americans of Japanese ancestry should be forcibly relocated from their homes on the West Coast, including all of California and parts of Oregon, Washington, and Arizona. The authorities were concerned that Japanese Americans would pass information about naval activities in important military cities, such as San Diego and Seattle, to the Japanese.

*Many Americans were alarmed by the surprise Japanese attack at Pearl Harbor on December 7, 1941. The attack caused widespread suspicion of the loyalty of Japanese Americans.*

# THE POWER OF THE PEOPLE

In 1944, a Japanese American named Fred Korematsu took Executive Order 9066 to the Supreme Court. Korematsu argued that it was unconstitutional to detain US citizens without trial. The court ruled against him by six votes to three. However, the order remained controversial long after the end of World War II. In 1980, civil rights groups persuaded President Jimmy Carter to hold an inquiry into the detention of Japanese Americans. The inquiry found that there was little evidence that Japanese Americans were disloyal to the US cause, and that their internment was the result of racism. In 1988, under President Ronald Reagan, the government officially apologized for internment. It also approved a payment of $20,000 in compensation to every survivor. The government eventually paid out about $1.6 billion to survivors and their descendants.

About 130,000 Japanese American citizens were moved from their homes. Many were sent to internment camps in the hostile desert, where they lived for the rest of the war. They lost their homes and businesses, and in many cases were left financially ruined. Most were second or third generation immigrants. Many had never even been to Japan. Some had family members who were serving in the US military and navy in the war against Japan.

> **WHAT DO YOU THINK?**
> Should Japanese Americans have had the same Constitutional protection from internment as other citizens? If not, why do you think they should have been treated differently?

## Civil Rights

Days before the end of World War II, Harry S. Truman became president. He issued executive orders to dismantle the wartime economy and to set up a committee to report on civil rights in the United States. Civil rights—particularly the rights of black Americans—would dominate politics for two decades. On July 26, 1948, Truman issued Executive Order 9981. It abolished racial discrimination in the United States armed forces. Previously, blacks and whites had served in different units, and black personnel had been prevented from gaining promotion. Truman judged change was needed to take advantage of the potential supply of black recruits for the military. The US Army was desegregated by late 1954.

That same year, the US Supreme Court ruled that **segregated** schooling was illegal. Schools throughout the country began to integrate. There was considerable resistance to integration in parts of the South, however. In 1957, in Little Rock, Arkansas, the governor used the

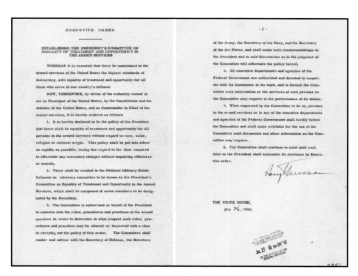

*Executive Order 9981 integrated the US armed forces. It followed Executive Order 8802, issued by FDR in 1941, which outlawed racial discrimination in the defense industry.*

*Soldiers of the 101st Airborne protect members of the Little Rock Nine as the students enter the previously white high school.*

national guard to prevent nine black students enrolling in a white school. President Dwight D. Eisenhower argued that, "Mob rule cannot be allowed to override the decisions of the courts." On September 24, 1957, he issued Executive Order 10730. It put the Arkansas National Guard under federal control and ordered the US Army to remove obstacles to the students' education. Eisenhower sent the crack 101st Airborne to guard the students against racist demonstrators.

## WHAT DO YOU THINK?

The governor of Arkansas complained about the "occupation" of the state after federal troops arrived in Little Rock. How would you justify ordering US troops to take action against US citizens?

# Chapter 4

# EXECUTIVE ORDERS
# TODAY

When President Barack Obama became president in 2009, he took more executive actions in his first two weeks than any other president. Most of those actions were not controversial. They included asking his staff to sign a pledge to maintain ethical behavior. Other actions drew more criticism, such as ordering the military to restrict their interrogation techniques in military prisons.

*When Barack Obama became president, he had the support of a Democratic Congress. In the later part of his presidency, however, he was often blocked by a Republican Congress.*

# Barack Obama

Obama's most controversial early action was to order the closure of the US military prison at Guantanamo Bay in Cuba. The prison was used to detain suspected **Islamist** terrorists and supporters, but it was controversial because inmates were detained there indefinitely without trial. Some prisoners claimed to be held mistakenly, while others said that they had been tortured.

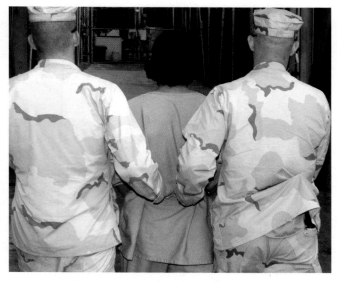

*The detention of suspected terrorists at Guantanamo Bay was widely criticized both in the United States and abroad.*

Obama had criticized the camp during his election campaign as reflecting badly on the reputation of the United States. However, despite Obama's executive order in 2009, the camp remained open throughout his presidency. Obama blamed Congress for holding up the closure of the prison, in such ways as refusing to authorize the money necessary to transfer the prisoners to camps within the United States. In return, critics of the president argued that he could have effectively shut the prison if he had actually been determined to do so. They argued that Obama's executive orders about Guantanamo Bay were more to do with appearances than with a real attempt to achieve change.

*Barack Obama's Climate Action Plan pledged that the United States would be a global leader in the fight to reduce carbon emissions and reduce global warming.*

## Pressing Issues

Throughout his presidency, Obama issued executive orders that reflected his concern about **climate change**. He began in 2009, with an order that asked federal agencies to improve their environmental impact. In 2013, Obama announced a Climate Action Plan to reduce carbon pollution. It was backed up by executive orders that federal agencies should help communities prepare for climate change and cut their own carbon emissions.

Another area in which Obama tried to change the law was gun control. In 2012, a gunman shot and killed 26 children and staff at Sandy Hook Elementary School in Newtown, Connecticut. Obama announced executive orders that included requiring firearms dealers to obtain licenses. In January 2016, he issued 18 executive actions about guns.

They included a call for background checks on people who wanted to buy guns. Critics of the move accused Obama of "**imperial** overreach." In fact, Obama's proposals made only minor changes to existing laws.

## A new president

In the election campaign of 2016, the Republican candidate Donald Trump criticized Obama's use of executive orders, particularly with relation to climate change and gun control.

*This memorial was set up at Newtown with the names of all the victims of the Sandy Hook shooting on December 14, 2012.*

## WHAT DO YOU THINK?

In 2018, parents from Sandy Hook announced their decision to prosecute a conspiracy theorist who claimed the massacre did not happen. Should promoting such theories be a crime? If so, why?

*Although President Trump could order federal agencies to build a wall to supplement current border defenses with Mexico, he relied on Congress to approve funding for construction.*

When he took office in January 2017, President Trump issued a series of executive orders. He ordered federal agencies to prepare to build a wall on the Mexican border. He cancelled Obama's order to close Guantanamo Bay, which, he said, held some "bad dudes." Trump also cancelled Obama's gun control measures and undid many of his orders about the environment. He argued that global warming was not scientifically proven. Trump said that environmental regulation harmed US businesses such as coal mining or steel production and unfairly increased their costs compared to those of competitors such as China and India.

## WHAT DO YOU THINK?

President Trump called global warming a "hoax." Most scientists believe that global warming is real. Why do you think the president ignores expert opinion?

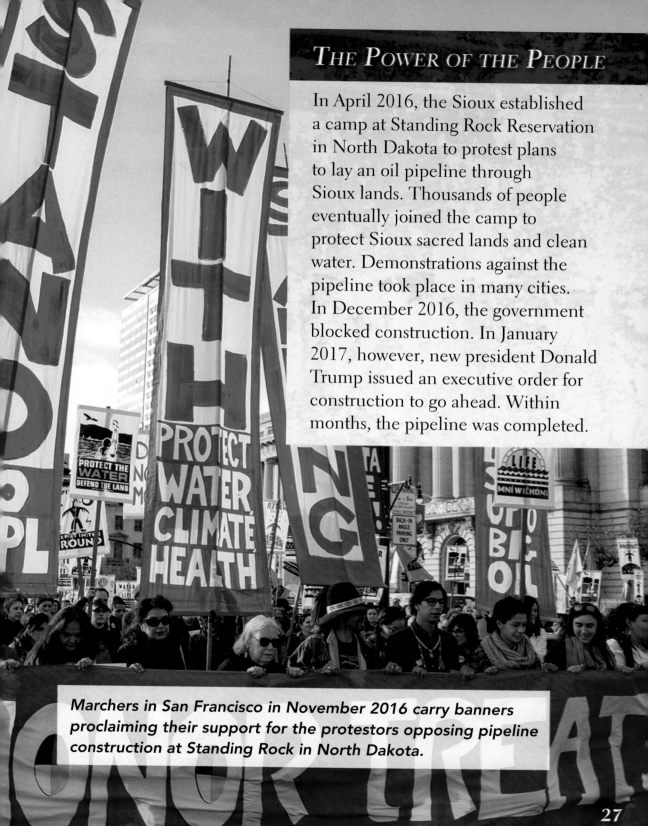

# THE POWER OF THE PEOPLE

In April 2016, the Sioux established a camp at Standing Rock Reservation in North Dakota to protest plans to lay an oil pipeline through Sioux lands. Thousands of people eventually joined the camp to protect Sioux sacred lands and clean water. Demonstrations against the pipeline took place in many cities. In December 2016, the government blocked construction. In January 2017, however, new president Donald Trump issued an executive order for construction to go ahead. Within months, the pipeline was completed.

*Marchers in San Francisco in November 2016 carry banners proclaiming their support for the protestors opposing pipeline construction at Standing Rock in North Dakota.*

Some of Donald Trump's executive orders were highly controversial. For example, in January 2017, he signed presidential memoranda to expand two oil pipelines. One, the Dakota Access Pipeline, crossed reservation land belonging to Native Americans, who objected to its construction. Trump also greatly reduced the size of two national parks in Utah to allow drilling for oil to take place.

Trump's most controversial executive order attempted to halt immigration from mainly Muslim countries. It caused

widespread public protest before it was overturned by the courts. A new version of the order later went into action, but was again subject to review in the courts for being unconstitutional.

*President Trump displays a signed executive order, watched by Vice President Mike Pence.*

---

**WHAT DO YOU THINK?**

Reservations are areas of land managed by Native American tribes. Native people claim the right to control their lands, not the federal government. What arguments might support their case?

## THE POWER OF THE PEOPLE

President Trump's first travel ban against immigrants from seven mainly Muslim countries went into effect on January 31, 2017. Thousands of Americans protested the executive order. Many immigration attorneys also offered more practical help. They headed to airports in order to offer free advice to immigrants arriving from the affected countries. The volunteers simply held up signs identifying themselves and reading "Here to Help." They helped people arriving get through immigration. The ban was overturned by the courts, but was revised and later issued again as a new executive order.

*Immigration lawyer Kapesh Patel holds a sign offering to assist travelers arriving at Los Angeles International Airport.*

# Chapter 5

# CONTROVERSIES AND DEBATES

Executive orders have often been controversial, but in many cases the controversy is more about party politics than about the principles of government. Republicans tend to support executive orders issued by Republican presidents but oppose those issued by Democratic presidents, and vice versa. In addition, many of the more than 13,000 executive orders have not been controversial at all. They include, for example, orders allowing named federal employees to remain in their jobs past the official retirement age.

However, some people are critical of the expansion of executive power in general. One of the presidents responsible for this expansion was Theodore Roosevelt in the early 1900s. Roosevelt issued more than 1,000 executive orders.

*Theodore "Teddy" Roosevelt was president from 1901 to 1909. He took many actions designed to protect the US wilderness and its unique wildlife and vegetation.*

*Roosevelt used an executive order to make the Grand Canyon a national monument on January 11, 1908.*

Roosevelt was concerned about preserving the environment. He created 150 national forests, 5 national parks, and 51 wildlife refuges, often through the use of executive orders. Roosevelt observed, "There was a great clamor that I was **usurping** legislative power… I did not usurp power, but I did greatly broaden the use of executive power."

In Roosevelt's view, any action that was not ruled out by the Constitution was fine for him to take. Other presidents had worked on the grounds that, unless the Constitution spelled out that they could do something, they could not. During the 1900s, Roosevelt's view became dominant.

## A Controversial Measure

Some executive orders have attracted great criticism. The Emancipation Proclamation of 1863 was opposed by Democrats in the North. They wanted the Union to be preserved, but with the continuation of slavery in the South. They greatly objected to Lincoln's decision to free the slaves.

## Recent Controversies

More recently, there has been particular controversy about executive orders concerned with gun control. President Obama's attempts to introduce checks for gun owners were criticized from both sides. Supporters of gun control argued that they did not go far enough. Supporters of the Second Amendment right to bear arms, however, argued that they represented illegal interference in the rights of citizens.

Immigration is another controversial subject. In 2012, President Obama introduced Deferred Action for Childhood Arrivals (DACA), a new policy contained in a memorandum issued by the Secretary of Homeland Security.

*President Trump argued that undoing many of President Obama's executive actions on climate change would encourage traditional US industries such as coal mining and steelmaking.*

DACA ordered that US Citizenship and Immigration Services grant exemption from deportation to illegal immigrants brought to the United States as children. Obama claimed DACA rewarded young people who made a positive contribution to US society, while freeing up authorities to prioritize deporting adult illegal immigrants and criminals. Opponents of the policy claimed that Obama had overstepped his presidential authority. In September 2017, President Trump announced his decision to end DACA.

*Protesters call for gun control by listing the numbers of victims in a series of mass shootings in the United States.*

## WHAT DO YOU THINK?

Do you think president Obama's DACA order overstepped his presidential authority? How do you think ending DACA will affect young immigrants who have made America their home?

President Trump's decision to end DACA was announced by Attorney General Jeff Sessions in September 2017. For some people, it was the first time they were really aware of DACA recipients, or Dreamers, and their vulnerable legal status. Demonstrations against ending the program were held throughout the country. Protestors staged a fast on Capitol Hill in Washington, D.C., while others marched down Fifth Avenue in New York City to Trump Tower, the president's private home. School students in Colorado staged a walkout. The protests did not remove the threat to the Dreamers, but they moved it high up the political agenda to ensure that politicians would have to come up with a solution to the problem.

*Demonstrators, including many Hispanic Americans, join a protest in San Francisco against President Trump's decision to end the DACA program.*

*Demonstrators in Manhattan march against President Trump's ban on immigrants from a number of Muslim-majority countries.*

President Trump said he wanted Congress to pass a Dream Act. This act would not only allow DACA recipients, known as Dreamers, to stay in the country. It would also allow them to become citizens—something not included under DACA. Many Americans supported the Dreamers. The president blamed Congress for being unable to reach an agreement to protect the Dreamers, although he still insisted he would overturn DACA. Activists were concerned that the Dreamers had become a bargaining chip in party politics. They looked to the president to take executive action to protect the Dreamers.

## WHAT DO YOU THINK?

President Trump argued that the Dreamers were a problem that Congress should solve. Congress seemed unable to do so. In such a case, should the president take executive action to resolve the issue?

# Chapter 6

# EXECUTIVE ORDERS
# AND YOU

The US political system places a lot of power in the hands of one individual, the president, but his or her power is supposed to be balanced by that of Congress and the courts. On his or her own, therefore, the president might seem to have only a limited ability to impact everyday life. Executive orders and other presidential actions mean that this is not the case. Decisions taken in the White House can have a direct impact on the lives of millions of Americans and non-Americans who come into contact with any form of government department or agency.

## Protecting the Environment

For young people in the United States, the chances are that their lives have already been impacted by executive orders in a number of ways. Many young people, for example, feel strongly about environmental issues. They might have supported Barack Obama's attempts to make federal agencies more environmentally efficient. Indirectly, this helped increase the emphasis on recycling in everyday life. Many cities and townships introduced their own limits on carbon restrictions and began to use less polluting vehicles for public transportation. Many communities rejected President Trump's decision to reverse Obama's actions, and continue to promote environmental policies.

# THE POWER OF THE PEOPLE

On March 28, 2017, President Trump signed an executive order instructing the Environmental Protection Agency (EPA) to rewrite federal rules on carbon emissions. He said this would encourage the coal mining industry. He also announced his intention to remove other environmental protections. In response, activists organized the People's Climate March on April 29. Marchers protested the change at 300 locations throughout the United States, including more than 200,000 people in Washington, D.C. In addition, many states and cities announced their intention to keep environmental protections in place. Individual Americans also continued to try to cut carbon emissions by, for example, using less fossil fuel.

*Recycling plastic and glass is an environmentally beneficial policy that is promoted by many local authorities. Many Americans recycle regardless of environmental laws.*

# Gun Control

Some people argue that the best way to achieve better gun control is through executive action. On February 14, 2018, a former student shot and killed 17 people at Marjory Stoneman Douglas High School in Parkland, Florida. Following the incident, students across the country joined protests calling for government action to prevent further school shootings.

*Wayne LaPierre, executive vice president of the National Rifle Association, is a campaigner against gun controls.*

There had been more than 300 school shootings in the United States since 2013. Congress was reluctant to act, however. In part, this reflected deep divisions in attitudes toward firearms in the United States. In part, it also reflects the political power of groups such as the National Rifle Association (NRA). In all, the NRA spent $54 million on getting supportive politicians elected in 2016 including $30 million on Donald Trump's presidential campaign.

Despite student protests, it was clear that Congress would not act. President Trump talked about taking executive action. Among other solutions, he suggested arming teachers to fight off shooters. Ultimately, he announced a ban on bump stocks, which increase the firing rate of rifles.

# The Immigration Issue

Life for many students is also greatly affected by immigration, which is one of the main areas of recent executive orders. Some people may have classmates who are Dreamers, and uncertain about their future. The fate of such immigrants is just one aspect of immigration control in the United States. Others include the possible construction of a wall along the US border with Mexico to stop illegal arrivals, and increased restrictions on the arrival of refugees and immigrants from mainly Muslim countries.

*Supporters of President Obama's DACA program gather in Washington, D.C., in April 2016.*

## WHAT DO YOU THINK?

Some people blame powerful groups such as the NRA for preventing any debate about gun control. The NRA gives financial support to many politicians. What might the NRA expect from those politicians in return?

Some people argue that the border wall and the immigration ban go against both the US Constitution and the country's history of welcoming immigrants from around the world. Other people argue that immigration should be limited both to protect the jobs of Americans and to help prevent drug crime and Islamist terrorism within the United States.

*Immigration and Customs Enforcement officers deport an illegal immigrant suspected of drug-related crime.*

Presidents Obama and Trump had different views of the priorities of immigration services. Obama believed they should be focused on removing criminal illegal immigrants. Trump instead instructed agencies to focus on deporting all illegal immigrants.

## WHAT DO YOU THINK?

The United States has a history of immigration. Most Americans today are descended from immigrants. Does that mean the United States should be more sympathetic than other countries toward immigrants?

# A Wide-Ranging Impact

The president's ability to direct the priorities of federal agencies gives him or her authority over many areas of life. From national parks to immigration policy, from gun control to public holidays, from climate control to the armed forces, executive orders can impact all Americans. They influence life at home and at school, as well as many forms of transportation. They can also help shape the economy, such as by setting up investigations into the role of labor unions and their powers. Many people object to particular executive orders—but they are usually supported by the voters who, after all, were responsible for electing the president who issues them.

*Executive orders potentially impact many aspects of life, such as the price of items in the grocery store.*

# Chapter 7

# GETTING INVOLVED

It might seem difficult for a citizen to have any influence on executive orders. In fact, people can use their vote to simply remove a president and elect a new one. It has been common for a new president to cancel executive orders issued by his predecessor. If there are executive actions you support or oppose, you can write to presidential

*Congress is the usual location for trying to influence US government policy—but not when it comes to executive orders.*

candidates to ask their opinions. On a state level, it is possible to do the same with governors. Executive actions can be powerful ways of enacting policies—but only if the man or woman behind them is in a position to defend them.

Every four years, the public gets a chance to judge the executive actions of the president at the ballot box. Be prepared by researching what actions a president has taken and what actions a candidate promises to take if elected.

## THE POWER OF THE PEOPLE

After the shooting at Marjory Stoneman Douglas High School in February 2018, students who had survived launched a Never Again MSD movement on Facebook. They held a Never Again rally in Fort Lauderdale, Florida, to campaign for changes to gun laws. Emma González, a senior at the school, was among half a dozen students who spoke at the rally. She and other students made frequent appearances in the media condemning politicians who took money from the NRA.

Students from Marjory Stoneman Douglas High School join a rally in Fort Lauderdale, Florida. Organizers of the rally included students who had hidden in cupboards to escape the shooting.

43

*The occupant of the White House is ultimately answerable to the American people at the polls every four years.*

## Making Yourself Heard

Even while a president is still in office, it is possible to take action against an executive order. Any citizen is entitled to write to the White House expressing his or her view of a particular action. In addition, it is possible to become involved in a campaign to challenge an executive order. One way is to find an interest group that is mounting a legal challenge by referring an executive order to the courts.

## WHAT DO YOU THINK?

US citizens have to be 18 years old to vote. Do you think more young people would be active in politics if the voting age was lowered? What other measures might encourage young people to get involved?

You could contact a group that shares your views and volunteer to help by raising money to pay legal costs or by leafleting or making telephone calls to raise public awareness about a particular issue.

It is also possible to join groups trying to get new executive actions issued rather than protesting those that already exist. Groups campaigning for increased gun control, for example, staged high-profile events in 2018, when students left their classrooms to join protests calling on President Trump to take steps to avoid school shootings. Other groups tried to persuade the president that climate change was a genuine threat to Americans and that he should reconsider dropping environmental legislation.

Such groups welcome volunteers who are willing to donate time to help their cause.

## Changing Policies

Executive orders are issued by presidents— but they do not emerge in a vacuum. They reflect the political priorities of a time. The best way to try to influence them is to become involved in activities that aim to shape those general political priorities.

*Americans cast their votes in a polling center in Ventura County, California, during the 2016 presidential election.*

# Glossary

**abolition:** the legal ending of slavery

**cabinet:** members of the executive branch of government who run departments of the government

**climate change:** a long-term change in Earth's climate caused in part by human activity such as burning fossil fuels

**federal agencies:** government organizations set up for a specific purpose, such as managing resources or safeguarding national security

**imperial:** related to an empire, emperor or empress

**internment:** confining someone as a prisoner for political or military reasons

**Islamist:** supporting extreme Islamic beliefs that call for the destruction of Western values

**judiciary:** the part of the government responsible for the legal system, including judges and courts of law

**legislature:** elected members of the government who have the power to make or change laws by voting

**policies:** courses of action adopted by a government or other influential body

**segregated:** divided on grounds such as race or sex

**separation of powers:** giving legislative, executive, and judicial powers of government to separate bodies

**tyranny:** government by an individual or small group with unlimited power to mistreat their subjects

**usurping:** illegally undermining or removing power from someone else

# For More Information

## Books

**Hirsch, Rebecca E.** *How the Executive Branch Works.* How the US Government Works. Minneapolis, MN: Core Library, 2015.

**Perritano, John.** *Little Rock Nine.* St. Louis, MO: Turtleback Books, 2018.

**Waxman, Laura Hamilton.** *Japanese American Internment Camps.* Heroes of World War II. Minneapolis, MN: Lerner Publishing Group, 2018.

## Websites

**Office of the Federal Register**
*https://www.federalregister.gov/executive-orders*
A list of all the executive orders issued since 1994, with links to the texts.

**Presidential Actions Archive**
*https://www.whitehouse.gov/presidential-actions/*
A list of presidential actions and executive orders, organized by issue.

Publisher's note to educators and parents: Our editors have carefully reviewed these websites to ensure that they are suitable for students. Many websites change frequently, however, and we cannot guarantee that a site's future contents will continue to meet our high standards of quality and educational value. Be advised that students should be closely supervised whenever they access the Internet.

# Index